Our Pitiful Metaphors

haibun

Jean LeBlanc

ISBN: 978-81-8253-829-0

First Edition: 2022
Rs. 200/-

Cyberwit.net
HIG 45 Kaushambi Kunj, Kalindipuram
Allahabad - 211011 (U.P.) India
http://www.cyberwit.net
Tel: +(91) 9415091004
E-mail: info@cyberwit.net

Printed at Vcore Connect LLP.

For The Writers' Roundtable
of Sussex County, New Jersey,
in our 20th year.
For all you have taught me,
poet friends and prose friends,
I thank you!

***

work it out for yourself: the difference between a mountain and the silhouette of a dancer taking into account kinetics and tectonics, gendered verbs, words of unknown origin, words yet to be.

to rid the world
(or so she says)
of strangling vines

Gravity from a Massive Star Bends Time

one hour back (enough time for a dream of good news) waking to regret knowing i am daring to hope

all day
one eulogy
after another

but no you say you want more how can you write a poem that tells us nothing

crumpled traffic cone
another snowplow thunders
through the night

coldest day of the year that's all you need to know records are made to be broken

ice fishing
don't stand too long in one spot
father tells us

variations on ache

and you confuse the memory of one marsh with another and lose an argument about blue spruce or tamarack (it was spruce) and you miss the leaving of the red-winged blackbirds you miss so much these days (it was tamarack)

lake rimmed with gold
the sun finds (burns?)
a break in the clouds

***

an added layer of glass and midnight at mid-afternoon and snow on the rose and the herbs dead in their pots and it was all supposed to be so all supposed to be

empty frames
where your face
used to

***

sometimes i take them one by one the polished stones and wonder was it water or wind (one so scarce now, one too plentiful) curling my hand around every silent story

petrified forest
a dream transports you
to this cold place

again i pick up smooth stones on a riverbank and put them into my pockets as if they are the treasure it has taken me sixty years of searching to find and they shall have a new home in a mundane spot on a mundane shelf and engage in a stone's silent longing for floodtime, for mossbed, for shadowcurl of fern

my usual elegance
a smudge of ink
from a worn-down nib

collage

desk scraps. how this paper takes the watercolor; how this paper doesn't. in one poem i replace hat with heart. the meaning does not change. poor choice of glue but it holds for now. do you want me to sit with you. yes but no. no good that we both. the old lure of commas dashes. shards in the newplowed. blue ones especially prized. scraps what my heart your heart can.

hawk circles the field
hawk circles
hawk

***

the herbs dead in their pots even the mint which is said to be immortal you know by how it fills the air when you walk on it on some streambank or outer edge of meadow but here even it succumbs (is it neglect if so it may help to know that's also a way of life)

arguing about
which river
to die a little by

instead of a funeral

send everyone who knew me everyone who cared to find one of these: bright wings in a blue sky / black feathers against the clouds / view of hills folded onto themselves / proof of wildflower: just one any one of which can be seen from any window in any season

the only
inconvenience
unplanted bulbs

Doctor's Appointment

a spine too stiff to sit a cough a slouch a confession a cast off on wheels a copay that cannot be met a poem northern lights a caldera

in this order:
mouth mask
disease

the silent ones the lost glasses the ones who wish to wait outside (should i have waited outside) if i knew i had an hour (if we all knew how much time)

from the exam room
overhearing
some else's good news

***

montage three crows blue sky red oak in your head you sing the snowbird song what is he talking about swords for making some glib point we need to elide just pass right over crows

never a paved road
your bearings in these hills
so easy to lose

***

for there to be narrative some sense must. this is not wartime no great strife of nations no catastrophe. just one death not even in the paper yet. too small too large to explain

autumn rain
some foolish bird singing
in the hedge

Christine de Pizan

died believing joan of arc would lead the french to victory after victory; just enough time to praise and thank her with sixty-one verses (may joan live that many years may each day's battle end with the sun's glow on her face may her fire always burn)

)within(

***

we inflict upon the cosmos our pitiful metaphors. i have lost so many meaningless items: bookmark / hair ornament / scarf / the measuring tape from the little sewing kit. somehow it seems easier now willing the moon to wax and wane. nightly pep talks through the window unless the clouds intervene.

all the crosswalks
getting a new coat
of little white lies

***

for a moment when she freezes i am able to study the skin just above her eye — all metaphor is pitiful — you don't mean pitiful she says you mean pathetic —

wait for the sparrow
to sing whitethroat, whitethroat,
whitethroat

Tell You

about the junco (they usually travel in flocks) alone finding shelter or maybe even bare ground to peck at under the car after the blizzard tell you about the crows looking as if they enjoy this cold crisp day tell you about the song of the wrens in the garden

year's end
another address
to delete

Watercolor

every word twice but why but why when it rains the headlights and taillights double the streetlights up from beneath a walker disappears in the din around the square as we say in this no-horse town

last
flower
drops
still
an
orchid

plagiarism

(a love story)

mimic mimic mim—
her notebooks full
of the words s[he] loved

*

gat[her]ing
up the pages he wants
to have [ ] by his side

*

it learns to speak!
ghost of the raven
in his dreams

*

how we can know
yet not know
mimic mimic mim—

*

old raven
on the telephone pole—
call me

*

write it out by hand to see how it poems

*

scavenger of words—
raven's cover photo
always young

*

l [imitation]
one disease
mimics another

*

the book at last
he held [her]
in his hands

*

how does this end—
furnace? shredder? landfill?
raven never tells

Angels

i don't believe in them i repeat as i cut out an angel almost shearing it of its golden curls scalloping the edges of the wings taking care with the halo every fold of gown and why am i cutting out an angel there is a pattern here, hands and eyes and one bare foot and wishing for wings

let everyone
utter keen excitement
[mindful if alone]

***

search for truth takes a backseat to domestic drama/coma look back and label it ineffable the enthuse of lust cut with smarm [blame someone else all cells replaced every seven years] one last burst of indignation over connotations then someone else dead now dead now dead

that shrub that forgets
and flowers in autumn—
stripped bare

And then

the world begins to end. Fire, flood, famine, plague—the classic scourges. Prophets as usual predict the present. Streets red with blood? Mobile morgues. A corpse in every home? Statistics crowd the bottom of the screen. We foresee the futility of dreams. Rue anemone. A swan on her nest.

before clouds move in
as always nighthawks
above it all

Hic Sunt Dracones

from where you watch behind the grassy hummocks something looks different—the she-wolf and her son too shimmery, more light than substance (no not light but shadow, though it hurts your eyes to look full on) and deep down you know it's a trick, a projection of some sort (magic, mindfuck, both) but you get greedy for one more dive into the monsters' lair for however much treasure can fit into your pockets. *it was a trick* your last full thought.

translate this poem
one knife blade
at a time

how to tell you how the light

ignores your cheekbone for your chin / falls both yellow and gray / owes its allegiance to neither moon nor sun / is sorry for the window between / loves the hillside / misses the birds / after all this time still has not learned where we hide our tears / will be here long after we

where are we, she asks
choosing a page and crossing
out the words

desires of the letterer

words without the letter “s” / creamy crescent strokes / dream of ogive arches / waking relief of bluntness / an alphabet in which it is always night / no new details in the letter “P” / endless supply of burnt umber / protection from weathering / unbroken edges / simple outlines / compound curves / as few strokes as possible / red sable brushes / law of uniformity / a T-square always true / accord between spur and bevel / no confusion of ornament / gold leaf that does as it is told

aitch is for heron
becomes a flattened
arch of wings

multiflora rose

even from this distance you can see the thorns solitary bluebird how can they [how can we] (whose idea was it anyway to have february follow january) overwinter the wind sweeps through here off the water between these hills seemed like a good idea at the time no such thing as too many roses

the weight of sky
recognized
for who we are

The Lost Painting

We meant to hang it when the wallpaper had been redone, but we never did. It went out with the rest of the clutter. It was rather ugly. It clashed with the sofa. Was it an original somebody? These modern painters never do learn to draw, do they.

sisters / sitters
one always portraiting
the other

Perhaps we gave it to the neighbors, that young couple who helped us that time the heat went out, taking in the dogs while we stayed in a hotel. They seemed to like it, poor dears. Their house was damaged by a falling tree in a storm the following summer. The strain of having to begin anew was too much for their marriage.

three-quarter pose
three tulips
reaching for her

Such a loss hardly matters. If no one cherished it enough, so much the better. No critic louder than time.

in each portrait
a splash of red
for life, for death

Ida

The one who is missing sends a beam of light in her place. Bright enough to turn night to day. Bright enough to shine down through decades—centuries, if need be. You can call it "truth," but "light" will do. It was her medium, after all—the things she could do with light. To do those things, she also needed to understand darkness. The one who is missing is not missing—merely standing in a shadow called sister.

who owns the light
their rivalry painted out
on canvas

Master of the Embroidered Foliage

He watches closely as his wife does her needlework. This is how he has learned to apply paint with a brush: stitch by stitch, he says to himself. A fine thread, the sharpest needle, patient fingers, steady hand. The light on Mary's face, the babe in her arms. Spring flowers at her feet. In the background, the shadow of those who do not see. A tapestry in oils. His wife approves.

unencumbered heart—
always off to the side
angels watching

It Begins as an Ordinary Visit

they bring a small gift, flowers or food. their health has improved. everyone is younger. somewhere a goldfinch sings. the river makes a wide turn and disappears in both directions. the sky does something with colors and clouds. these is no talk of books, but then there never was. the room is tidy, generic. you'd think there'd be so much to say. a bird they once saw. the song it sang. singing meets silence, and the two are one.

it feels as if
they have never left
are always leaving

because eyes (tears)

a secret language written on the face in invisible tracks of long-ago dried tears but you know this already and know it well so how can it be secret (because we cannot see our own except in mirrors)

learning to read
the book always
upside-down

the secret keeps itself unless you have made a long and careful study of each tear and how it finds its way down your cheek or from eye to ear (the geometry of face)

and lips also know
though tongue's a quick
eraser

and so we drink in this entire dictionary of self and who we are is mineral residue (not quite really there always)

infinity
holding the 8 sideways
your eyes

Resolutions

Light exemplifies us. Kiss every mannequin into animation. Link emptiness, unused keys, early mornings in agreement. Listen: endeavor, unify, ken, expect, make, insist, aver.

winter heron
two miles out
and back

Limit excess unless kind. Eschew most inane articulations.

January day
almost bird
on almost reed

Lithe estuary, utility kingdoms. Each meander-inspired artifice. Look: evidence! Usually knowledge ekes meaning instead (always).

briars thorns ivy
how we lose ourselves
in the woods

Disembodied, a Voice

i.

but first we should agree on a definition of skin: that on which all desire / that under which resides / that through which one becomes little by little the other

agon(y)ou again a way of life a snow-filled cloud

ii.

snow virga driving back sitting as close as to keep warm we said no birds we laughed apologies to the crows not knowing our final winter trying to catch snowflakes from a distant cloud

thorns you whispered
(strange how soft the word is
in one's mouth)

iii.

climbing roses divinity in the garden a petal the silk of your dress laughing at thorns even as they snag tall shadow among tall shadows scissors in hand every earnest tendril of belief intertwined us

wordum wrixlan
you know the petals
from the sepals

iv.

i am a key. i was lost, and no one even knew to look for me. now i am wishful thinking. now i wear the patina of disuse. in your hand i warmed quickly. now i describe the mirror image of nothing

ungelic is us
i threw you—us—
overboard

v.

once more into the furnace the glassblower's breath within me the jacks at my neck and then this fragile afterlife of all things formed entirely out of hope

image/no image
the discipline of mind
to freeze you out

vi.

disembodied, a voice (the body disenvoiced, distouched) comes to me chair behind chair the newest way to unsee what is there panicanswer bladeword after bladeword and again, agonsilence disembodied (walk around this unwalkable room) hatevoice my own

amica ripae
all the water in the world
between us always

vii.

your parting gifts to me: coin with the face of some old king a pack of sewing needles lessons in how to reconcile the limits of a mind I loved how to traverse an afterlife that promises everything other than

it is this simple:
picture snow where once
our footprints

Two Late Self-Portraits

i.

palette: gray, plum. always holding something. brushes—always holding brushes. brushwork. one can hear the word as if she were whispering: brushwork. but it was second nature [no, first] by then, brush tip meeting canvas. brush tip knowing canvas. canvas knowing back.

even indoors
an oversized hat—each eye
a shadowed thing

ii.

in this one i shall show my eyes. behind glasses. same large hat, but i raise my chin so the shadow pulls back, pulls up. an old woman appears on the canvas. darkness is no longer simply background. if you are young you have already stopped looking.

crumpled paper
one more afternoon
of new snow

in his own way

[most tragic words] he loved her. lifelong companions. studios side by side. his last portrait of her at her easel, one shoe half-off. the arch of her foot [a tender, funny detail] yes he loved her. in his own way [not hers]. not enough. not enough.

all these brushes
bristles dry and loose
as if they'd never

consciousness: the musical

the neuroscientists muscle in on the territory of the philosophers and somebody dissects somebody and somebody sings *no that's not where you'll find it* and someone else sings *how do i know i know* and they dance (it's a mock-fight) and a psychologist (or maybe a poet) offers someone some advice and some publish and others perish (someone dies in someone's arms) while the ones remaining sing about the irony of only knowing what it ain't

storm forecast:
a pair of cardinals
plus extra snowbirds

novel in search of a plot

the protagonist reveals in an interior monologue that he hates the use of interior monologues. we have come this far and suddenly what little plot had borne us along. secondary characters disintegrate on the page. the one he should have kissed when the two of them were alone in the kitchen. time alone was never found. passive voice. cliché. outside a wind storm the sky orange

a pro forma turn
of a pro forma page
no spine to speak of

abstract landscape

it may be the field you pass these days every curl of every leaf of grass it may be sky it may be old snow underfoot reflection of tree in open water sudden shelf of ice where low sun never it may be hillside it may be a bird or a shadow of bird

a trick of light
deer in the road
same spot each time

outsider

loneliness stitched into every seam (every seem) and poor stitching too the needle's path straying far off course over impossible (impassable) mountains across oceans as if trying to finish off the quilt of this world and just sewing, sewing (what poor soul would call that poor)

every button lost
a penny a secret
and vulner(able)

conversation over a hill of snow

i am lonely she says (i imagine) i am alone i reply (silently) i am reluctant to move from this spot (a glance downward) you are in my way (shuffling of feet) i would be glad to help (actually voiced) i would be glad to get on with the job (implied) too many not enough words (she repeats most) (i repeat) but thank you but thank you

she folds the sidewalk
and presses a sharp crease
origami flower

Texas Falls

Nowhere near Texas. A northern stream that has sliced through schist and smoothed the sides. A little help at the start from a glacier. Only for these several yards. It's the depth that's impressive. Forest floor, forest floor, a tangle of exposed hemlock root, then hypothetical you would (briefly) wonder where the ground went, why all these little ferns are waving good-bye.

de mal en pis
from the top of the page
to the bottom

***

Nostalgia doesn't suit the aging poet. It's a lumpy suit, all the wrong sizes, baggy at the shoulders, tight around the waist, the button straining. Sleeves too short. Frumpy cuffs showing too much ankle. O the songs of my teen-aged years, it wails, o where are they now, where is that radio static and the records that skip, records that skip, records that skip, or better still the harmonies on city sidewalks beneath a streetlight. When all else refuses to reveal meaning, write a poem about the songs of your youth. Especially if you yourself could never sing.

a snowpile blocks
the covered bridge, even in
this modern rain

see the white space on this page:

all the words i did not waste on you the breath i did not expend trying to convince you of the stories i did tell but you would not listen and i refused to repeat the thoughts i kept to myself when you were having it out with solipsism

painting again
his grave too far away
to stop me

the year we blew up the moon

some sort of accident caused by something at one of the lunar bases. it took a while but eventually earth's erstwhile tide pools no longer smelled of salty death and sea gulls ate the last of the periwinkles and we all have dried starfish to remind us of when the oceans pulsed and how words such as "ebb" and "neap" were more than crossword puzzle oddities. most of us over a certain age can rarely bring ourselves to look up at what passes for the night sky

please, spider,
there are darker corners
of this house

a note on the type face

The font used in this book was designed by someone who spent countless hours in a quiet room. The subtle embellishment of two or three of the letters was inspired by the cooing of imaginary doves in an imaginary dovecote. A few new letters have been added; a few others, promoted in rank. This designer also standardized, in the 1820s, the way the sky turns bluer at dusk. If you stare at the print on this page long enough, you will see it become blue, deeper and deeper.

the wrens have returned
or else some other
silent letter bird

ocular migraine

a little piece of route 80 dissolves. if i hold my head just so i can see the painted lines and the car ahead of me. i remind myself not to be distracted by the unwoven portion of my field of vision. i want to stare at it, appreciate this new way of softening the world.

one haiku away
a swan rears up
in the breakdown lane

***

old photos taken in full sun women's faces lost to the shadows cast by their hats a cheekbone or a chin all there is to remind us of who they were

the stream and
these cherry blossoms
gravity fed

***

crow and full moon meet: maple trees leafed out the mornings warm
a body they call a lake but shallow enough to walk across

old photos of birds
just what poets do
when words

***

i loved the painting because you loved it. i bought the same cheap print and taped it to a wall. i imagined a life for you that i would have liked to have lived. we had secret names for one another. one day i helped you clean your room, draped a sweater over the back of a chair. you reversed our secret names, called me the one that made no sense on me. forty-five years later you get it right

still whole but soon
just a torn strip
of eyes

Carcass Creek

little broken sticks thrown in will float who knows where and the name—you don't need to ask, you can think of hundreds of plausible stories as the reason for that—dappled sunlight little sticks on their way (memory on its way in little broken) we, we are the carcass, each of us

roadside shrine
a tree nicked too many times
by the snowplow

advice

avoid italics, questions, exclamations, dashes, semi-colons, rhyme, free verse, interior monologue, dialogue, adjectives, adverbs, omniscient point of view, analogy, allegory, wordiness, minimalism, ellipsis, et cetera, emotion, romance, desperation, earthquake, tedium, memory, imagination, train schedules, abstractions, images, symbols, writing.

rhetorical q:
birches and beneath them
deep snow

the taste of denial

stale and dry right behind the lower front teeth almost-but-not-quite fetid in that sweet way like autumn refuse after rain pursued by that rot in gut and sternum and scapula and spine and carotid and

a mind gone hard
stopped by the long shadow
of the crossing guard

languages

we speak stone. we speak rain. we speak glass. we speak rust. we speak sand. we translate bone into fire but never fire to bone. we translate light into anything but light. we go on translating mute to muter, trying to learn the language of bone and light (but those languages are forgotten as soon as we know what it was we wanted to say)

where the catbird sings
a dead end
from both directions

island of the last living birds

the ruby-throated hummingbird, its species once so common, looks around from its perch, its back to the rising sun / it is a cold morning following a colder night / a yellow warbler sings to itself / nesting material is abundant here, as are flowers / a swarm of gnats thrives as the surface of the water warms / the air is slow to warm, and even when it does / we will listen to old recordings of songs and calls / then return to silence / and look, there goes a

not a meadow
what synonym for clearing
would you prefer

systrophe in an outdated idiom

stalker of dawn (pathetic fallacy) feather of ink written on sky (magical thinking) speaker of truth teller of lies (projection) be-deviller of hawks bedeviled in return (paradox) bone picker tongue thief eulogy prompter elegy scribbler enigma shadow (scesis onomaton) complete and utter devastation (pleonasm and cliché)

chooses to replace gone with never

november

twisted up the poem so bad it means. spiral bound we make our way in all. hemlock grove naming every storm these trees have seen. sunlight in the woods my shadow stumbles.

wild orchids gone to seed
how does this work
this meaning thing

What We Learn from Our Mistakes

The red-winged blackbirds have chosen poor nesting sites this year: one at the base of the footbridge, where a watersnake will eat the eggs, and one in a sedge hummock an easy step or two through shallow water for the fox. The female sends up an alarm, perches nearby with a drooping wing, but do you really believe snake and fox will be distracted. Time rarely permits a second brood.

why the key won't turn
as always morning clouds
obscure the sun

Context Clues

A memory too alsmingstrup to be shared. I am durnstipplefied, or else I would accompany you. What happened there was loudapurn, tending toward tragic. Happy, shobraiched, immeljayed. To see an enellmonter, ask an expert. No, the opposite of travingstun: archiped, molten, vexed. All this margin, when even the prose seems convilliconned. Senolibria, without which all is numeralimon. Mixed media: grave askings, neep peelings, pinking shears. I disjunctive in the furthest corner from another's unknowable unfathom.

dance through the pain
what other choice
for empternity?

a blue dress

[lily dale, summer, 2019]

but what if your photos were black and white, if there were photos at all / sounds fancy, but could be a blue cotton house dress, a plain everyday shift / sky blue, faded blue, navy / or by the time you were in the picture just squares of fabric in a quilt maybe that's where you would remember it / so who here had a mother aunt grandmother who [never] wore blue / someone wants to talk to you now

one damselfly
finds a sunbeam on my hand
all sepia tones

photo:

torn almost in two when it was removed from the album / why did we keep those old albums the bulk of them like no other book / well an atlas maybe / the atlas of everyone we knew whose names / why bother to write down / or which front steps which lake which picnic spot / people and places with no

her name
a curl
in faded ink

a journey

on the painted scroll, eighteen feet long, a traveler appears. same traveler, in several different places along the scroll, as if we see his journey as a whole, or as if we travel with him. the path is long and steep. where it is steepest, stairs have been carved into the mountain. his joy is our joy at the little way-stations: a cup of tea, a nap, a dragonfly carried by a summer storm up into this thin air.

all the elements
at once—one umbrella
for the two of us

two photographs

it is a simple photograph, a simple composition. a figure in a blue habit—an old-school nun—walks through the door of a cathedral. her face already in shadows. her eyes already on the next life. everything else is stone. what isn't stone is air.

smiles back at us
in the red sweater
she'll be buried in

***

just north of austerlitz, new york, on the taconic state parkway, a traveler gets a glimpse of a sculpture park that features a giant stone head staring out over the rolling hills in sun, rain, snow, a wise or surprised visage depending on light and shadows and the traveler must keep moving, must leave this moment behind

motel mirror
a night of unexpected
reflections

***

In his universe there can be anti-anything. Anti-trees. Anti-slippers. Anti-windows. I do not ask where he goes for shade, for warmth in winter, for clarity. This traffic rushing by, he says. I am anti-traffic. Opposite, not against. Other, not con. As far from as possible. More than possible. Curse all asphalt, curse this anti-river.

fragile begonia
break off whichever
syllable you choose

prediction

tamp down the sun / this patch of sunlight your last / that cheap angel you left behind / what the spirits forget to tell us / no one sees this coming / the fortune teller forgets the fortune part: / you will walk and walk

this ache
this pain
a syzygy of noir

write me something

something medieval she says. something like that poem you love about the man hiding on an island and the woman who loves him but has let someone else marry her because it was her only way to survive

an intersection painted
with instructions—
suddenly three lanes

or that other story about the woman who takes her baby and walks off into the swamp and is never seen again

our week beachcombing
at low tide
for sand dollars

that's late nineteenth century american, not medieval, i say. same thing, she says. so here's the thing: we're all pretty much interchangeable. reliquaries are made of this. behold, the left index finger knuckle of saint catherine, her last gesture to point toward heaven as the wheel broke every bone . . . you get the picture. anyone's knuckle, anyone's. we are all saints, or at least our bones are all sacred, any piece of any one of us could end up on some altar. or as evidence of a crime not actually committed. here, my fine lady, the thigh bone of the one you spill tears for, picked clean by crows. come with me and i'll let you bury it—him—at the edge of this fen. we go our separate ways, then, wulf. your island you will never leave. my island, my memory. but it could have been anyone's femur. he could be watching her now, from behind this story

catbird's predictions:
in one hour, sunrise
and this poem

origami

if i had any skill at it i'd fold a swan. an iris. a cease-fire, one that would then unfold itself into lasting peace.

the low hum
of the watercooler
too late for birdsong

fold me a metaphor that isn't pitiful. a peony that spring rain doesn't thrash against the ground. love that doesn't end up an anagram of recriminations (in cremation, sir). all of it, including ourselves, a flammable art.

up to my thighs
in waterlily—
open, open

www.ingramcontent.com/pod-product-compliance
Lightning Source LLC
Chambersburg PA
CBHW022202160726
48282CB00024B/292
* 9 7 8 8 1 8 2 5 3 8 2 9 0 *